50 Crafting Cocktail Making Recipes for Home

By: Kelly Johnson

Table of Contents

- Old Fashioned
- Negroni
- Mojito
- Margarita
- Manhattan
- Martini
- Moscow Mule
- Whiskey Sour
- Daiquiri
- Cosmopolitan
- Mint Julep
- Mai Tai
- French 75
- Pisco Sour
- Paloma
- Sazerac
- Bloody Mary
- Espresso Martini
- Tom Collins
- Gimlet
- Dark 'n' Stormy
- Aperol Spritz
- Sidecar
- White Russian
- Caipirinha
- Mojito
- Piña Colada
- Irish Coffee
- Blue Lagoon
- Long Island Iced Tea
- Tequila Sunrise
- Sex on the Beach
- Hurricane
- Singapore Sling
- Vodka Martini

- Whiskey Smash
- Rum Punch
- White Lady
- Zombie
- Bellini
- French Martini
- Rob Roy
- Brandy Alexander
- Black Russian
- Irish Mule
- Aviation
- Godfather
- Boulevardier
- Grasshopper
- Dark and Stormy

Old Fashioned

Ingredients:

- 2 oz (60 ml) bourbon or rye whiskey
- 1 sugar cube (or 1/2 tsp of granulated sugar)
- 2-3 dashes Angostura bitters
- Orange peel
- Ice cubes

Instructions:

1. Place the sugar cube in an Old Fashioned glass (or a rocks glass).
2. Add the Angostura bitters directly onto the sugar cube.
3. Muddle the sugar cube and bitters together until the sugar is dissolved.
4. Add a large ice cube or a few regular ice cubes to the glass.
5. Pour the bourbon or rye whiskey over the ice.
6. Stir gently to combine.
7. Express the oils from the orange peel over the drink by holding it over the glass and giving it a twist to release the oils.
8. Rub the orange peel around the rim of the glass and drop it into the drink.
9. Optionally, garnish with a cherry.
10. Enjoy your classic Old Fashioned!

Feel free to adjust the amount of sugar and bitters to suit your taste preferences.

Cheers!

Negroni

Ingredients:

- 1 oz (30 ml) gin
- 1 oz (30 ml) Campari
- 1 oz (30 ml) sweet vermouth
- Orange twist or slice, for garnish
- Ice cubes

Instructions:

1. Fill a mixing glass or cocktail shaker with ice cubes.
2. Pour the gin, Campari, and sweet vermouth into the shaker.
3. Stir the ingredients well for about 30 seconds to chill and properly dilute the drink.
4. Strain the mixture into an old-fashioned glass filled with ice.
5. Garnish your Negroni with an orange twist or slice.
6. Serve and enjoy your classic Negroni!

For a twist, you can try using different types of gin or adjusting the ratios of the ingredients to suit your taste. Cheers!

Mojito

Ingredients:

- 2 oz (60 ml) white rum
- 1 oz (30 ml) fresh lime juice
- 2 teaspoons (8 g) granulated sugar
- 6-8 fresh mint leaves, plus extra for garnish
- Club soda (to top up)
- Ice cubes
- Lime wedges, for garnish

Instructions:

1. In a cocktail shaker or a mixing glass, muddle the mint leaves, lime juice, and sugar together until the mint is fragrant and the sugar is dissolved.
2. Add the white rum to the shaker.
3. Fill the shaker with ice cubes and shake well to chill the mixture.
4. Strain the mixture into a highball glass filled with ice cubes.
5. Top up the glass with club soda.
6. Stir gently to combine.
7. Garnish your Mojito with a sprig of fresh mint and a lime wedge.
8. Serve and enjoy your refreshing Mojito!

You can adjust the sweetness and tartness of the Mojito by varying the amount of sugar and lime juice according to your preference. Cheers!

Margarita

Ingredients:

- 2 oz (60 ml) silver tequila
- 1 oz (30 ml) triple sec or Cointreau
- 1 oz (30 ml) fresh lime juice
- Salt (for rimming, optional)
- Lime wedge, for garnish
- Ice cubes

Instructions:

1. If desired, rim the edge of a margarita glass with salt. To do this, rub a lime wedge around the rim of the glass, then dip the rim into a shallow dish of salt.
2. Fill a cocktail shaker with ice cubes.
3. Pour the tequila, triple sec (or Cointreau), and fresh lime juice into the shaker.
4. Shake the ingredients well for about 15-20 seconds to chill the mixture.
5. Strain the mixture into the prepared margarita glass filled with ice cubes.
6. Garnish your Margarita with a lime wedge.
7. Serve and enjoy your classic Margarita!

For variations, you can try adding fruit flavors such as strawberry or mango for a fruity twist. Adjust the sweetness and tartness by altering the amount of triple sec and lime juice to suit your taste preferences. Cheers!

Manhattan

Ingredients:

- 2 oz (60 ml) rye whiskey or bourbon
- 1 oz (30 ml) sweet vermouth
- 2 dashes Angostura bitters
- Maraschino cherry, for garnish (optional)
- Orange twist, for garnish (optional)
- Ice cubes

Instructions:

1. Fill a mixing glass or cocktail shaker with ice cubes.
2. Pour the rye whiskey (or bourbon), sweet vermouth, and Angostura bitters into the shaker.
3. Stir the ingredients well for about 30 seconds to chill and properly dilute the drink. If you prefer a slightly lighter and more aromatic Manhattan, you can stir for less time.
4. Strain the mixture into a chilled cocktail glass.
5. Garnish your Manhattan with a maraschino cherry and/or an orange twist, if desired.
6. Serve and enjoy your classic Manhattan!

For variations, you can try using different types of whiskey or bourbon to give your Manhattan a unique flavor profile. Adjust the ratio of whiskey to vermouth according to your taste preferences. Cheers!

Martini

Ingredients:

- 2 oz (60 ml) gin or vodka
- 1/2 oz (15 ml) dry vermouth
- Lemon twist or olive, for garnish
- Ice cubes

Instructions:

1. Fill a mixing glass or cocktail shaker with ice cubes.
2. Pour the gin (or vodka) and dry vermouth into the shaker.
3. Stir the ingredients well for about 30 seconds to chill and properly dilute the drink. If you prefer a slightly lighter and more aromatic Martini, you can stir for less time.
4. Strain the mixture into a chilled martini glass.
5. Garnish your Martini with a lemon twist or olive, if desired.
6. Serve and enjoy your classic Martini!

For variations, you can try using different types of gin or vodka to give your Martini a unique flavor profile. You can also adjust the ratio of gin (or vodka) to vermouth according to your taste preferences. Cheers!

Moscow Mule

Ingredients:

- 2 oz (60 ml) vodka
- 1/2 oz (15 ml) fresh lime juice
- 4-6 oz (120-180 ml) ginger beer
- Lime wedge, for garnish
- Ice cubes

Instructions:

1. Fill a copper mug or highball glass with ice cubes.
2. Pour the vodka and fresh lime juice over the ice.
3. Top up the glass with ginger beer.
4. Stir gently to combine.
5. Garnish your Moscow Mule with a lime wedge.
6. Serve and enjoy your refreshing Moscow Mule!

The copper mug is traditional for serving Moscow Mules and helps keep the drink cool, but you can use any glass if you don't have one. Adjust the amount of ginger beer and lime juice according to your taste preferences. Cheers!

Whiskey Sour

Ingredients:

- 2 oz (60 ml) whiskey (bourbon or rye)
- 3/4 oz (22 ml) fresh lemon juice
- 1/2 oz (15 ml) simple syrup
- Optional: Egg white (for a frothy texture)
- Lemon twist or cherry, for garnish
- Ice cubes

Instructions:

1. Fill a cocktail shaker with ice cubes.
2. Pour the whiskey, fresh lemon juice, and simple syrup into the shaker.
3. Optionally, add the egg white to the shaker for a frothy texture (this is traditional but optional).
4. Shake the ingredients vigorously for about 15-20 seconds to chill the mixture and create froth if using egg white.
5. Strain the mixture into a rocks glass filled with ice cubes.
6. Garnish your Whiskey Sour with a lemon twist or cherry.
7. Serve and enjoy your classic Whiskey Sour!

Feel free to adjust the sweetness and tartness of the Whiskey Sour by altering the amount of simple syrup and lemon juice according to your taste preferences. Cheers!

Daiquiri

Ingredients:

- 2 oz (60 ml) white rum
- 3/4 oz (22 ml) fresh lime juice
- 1/2 oz (15 ml) simple syrup
- Lime wheel or wedge, for garnish
- Ice cubes

Instructions:

1. Fill a cocktail shaker with ice cubes.
2. Pour the white rum, fresh lime juice, and simple syrup into the shaker.
3. Shake the ingredients vigorously for about 15-20 seconds to chill the mixture.
4. Strain the mixture into a chilled cocktail glass.
5. Garnish your Daiquiri with a lime wheel or wedge.
6. Serve and enjoy your classic Daiquiri!

For variations, you can try using flavored syrups or adding fruit purees for different flavor profiles. Adjust the sweetness and tartness by altering the amount of simple syrup and lime juice according to your taste preferences. Cheers!

Cosmopolitan

Ingredients:

- 1 1/2 oz (45 ml) vodka
- 1/2 oz (15 ml) triple sec or Cointreau
- 1/2 oz (15 ml) fresh lime juice
- 1/2 oz (15 ml) cranberry juice
- Lime twist or wedge, for garnish
- Ice cubes

Instructions:

1. Fill a cocktail shaker with ice cubes.
2. Pour the vodka, triple sec (or Cointreau), fresh lime juice, and cranberry juice into the shaker.
3. Shake the ingredients vigorously for about 15-20 seconds to chill the mixture.
4. Strain the mixture into a chilled martini glass.
5. Garnish your Cosmopolitan with a lime twist or wedge.
6. Serve and enjoy your classic Cosmopolitan!

Feel free to adjust the tartness and sweetness of the Cosmopolitan by altering the amount of lime juice and cranberry juice according to your taste preferences. Cheers!

Mint Julep

Ingredients:

- 2 oz (60 ml) bourbon
- 1/2 oz (15 ml) simple syrup
- 4-6 fresh mint leaves, plus extra for garnish
- Crushed ice
- Mint sprig, for garnish

Instructions:

1. In a julep cup or rocks glass, lightly muddle the fresh mint leaves and simple syrup to release the mint oils.
2. Fill the glass with crushed ice, packing it down gently.
3. Pour the bourbon over the crushed ice.
4. Stir gently to mix the ingredients and chill the drink.
5. Top up the glass with more crushed ice if needed.
6. Garnish your Mint Julep with a sprig of fresh mint.
7. Serve and enjoy your refreshing Mint Julep!

The Mint Julep is traditionally served in a silver or pewter cup, but any sturdy glass will do. Feel free to adjust the sweetness by adding more or less simple syrup to suit your taste preferences. Cheers!

Mai Tai

Ingredients:

- 1 1/2 oz (45 ml) white rum
- 1/2 oz (15 ml) dark rum
- 3/4 oz (22 ml) orange curaçao
- 3/4 oz (22 ml) lime juice
- 1/2 oz (15 ml) orgeat syrup
- 1/2 oz (15 ml) simple syrup
- Pineapple spear, cherry, and mint sprig for garnish (optional)
- Crushed ice

Instructions:

1. Fill a cocktail shaker with ice cubes.
2. Pour the white rum, dark rum, orange curaçao, lime juice, orgeat syrup, and simple syrup into the shaker.
3. Shake the ingredients vigorously for about 15-20 seconds to chill the mixture.
4. Fill a rocks glass with crushed ice.
5. Strain the cocktail mixture into the glass over the crushed ice.
6. Optionally, garnish your Mai Tai with a pineapple spear, cherry, and mint sprig.
7. Serve and enjoy your classic Mai Tai!

The Mai Tai is a tropical cocktail with a perfect balance of sweet, tart, and boozy flavors. Feel free to adjust the sweetness and tartness by adding more or less orgeat syrup and lime juice according to your taste preferences. Cheers!

French 75

Ingredients:

- 1 1/2 oz (45 ml) gin
- 1/2 oz (15 ml) fresh lemon juice
- 1/2 oz (15 ml) simple syrup
- Champagne or sparkling wine, chilled
- Lemon twist, for garnish

Instructions:

1. Fill a cocktail shaker with ice cubes.
2. Pour the gin, fresh lemon juice, and simple syrup into the shaker.
3. Shake the ingredients vigorously for about 15-20 seconds to chill the mixture.
4. Strain the mixture into a chilled champagne flute.
5. Top up the glass with champagne or sparkling wine.
6. Gently stir to combine.
7. Garnish your French 75 with a lemon twist.
8. Serve and enjoy your elegant French 75!

The French 75 is a delightful combination of gin, citrus, and bubbles, perfect for celebrations or any special occasion. Adjust the sweetness by adding more or less simple syrup to suit your taste preferences. Cheers!

Pisco Sour

Ingredients:

- 2 oz (60 ml) Pisco
- 1 oz (30 ml) fresh lime juice
- 3/4 oz (22 ml) simple syrup
- 1 egg white
- Angostura bitters, for garnish
- Ice cubes

Instructions:

1. Fill a cocktail shaker with ice cubes.
2. Pour the Pisco, fresh lime juice, simple syrup, and egg white into the shaker.
3. Shake the ingredients vigorously for about 15-20 seconds to emulsify the egg white and chill the mixture.
4. Strain the mixture into a rocks glass filled with ice cubes.
5. Add a few drops of Angostura bitters on top of the foam.
6. Optionally, use a toothpick or skewer to create a decorative pattern in the foam.
7. Serve and enjoy your classic Pisco Sour!

The Pisco Sour is a refreshing and tangy cocktail with a silky foam top. Adjust the sweetness by adding more or less simple syrup to suit your taste preferences. Cheers!

Paloma

Ingredients:

- 2 oz (60 ml) tequila (preferably blanco or reposado)
- 1/2 oz (15 ml) fresh lime juice
- Pinch of salt
- Grapefruit soda (such as Jarritos or Squirt)
- Lime wedge, for garnish
- Salt or Tajín (optional, for rimming)
- Ice cubes

Instructions:

1. If desired, rim a highball glass with salt or Tajín. To do this, rub a lime wedge around the rim of the glass, then dip the rim into a shallow dish of salt or Tajín.
2. Fill the glass with ice cubes.
3. Pour the tequila and fresh lime juice over the ice.
4. Add a pinch of salt to the glass.
5. Top up the glass with grapefruit soda.
6. Stir gently to combine.
7. Garnish your Paloma with a lime wedge.
8. Serve and enjoy your refreshing Paloma!

The Paloma is a simple and refreshing cocktail with a perfect balance of tartness, sweetness, and a hint of salt. Adjust the sweetness by using more or less grapefruit soda or adding a splash of simple syrup if desired. Cheers!

Sazerac

Ingredients:

- 2 oz (60 ml) rye whiskey
- 1/4 oz (7 ml) absinthe or absinthe substitute (such as Pernod or Herbsaint)
- 1 sugar cube
- 3 dashes Peychaud's bitters
- Lemon twist, for garnish
- Ice cubes

Instructions:

1. Fill an old-fashioned glass with ice cubes to chill it, then set it aside.
2. In a separate mixing glass, muddle the sugar cube with the Peychaud's bitters until the sugar is dissolved.
3. Add the rye whiskey to the mixing glass with the muddled sugar and bitters.
4. Fill the mixing glass with ice cubes and stir well to chill the mixture.
5. Discard the ice from the chilled old-fashioned glass.
6. Add the absinthe to the glass, swirling it around to coat the interior, then discard any excess absinthe.
7. Strain the chilled whiskey mixture into the prepared glass.
8. Express the oils from a lemon twist over the drink by holding it over the glass and giving it a twist to release the oils. Then, drop the twist into the drink as a garnish.
9. Serve and enjoy your classic Sazerac!

The Sazerac is a historic cocktail with a unique flavor profile, combining the warmth of rye whiskey with the herbal notes of absinthe and the aromatic complexity of Peychaud's bitters. Cheers!

Bloody Mary

Ingredients:

- 1 1/2 oz (45 ml) vodka
- 3 oz (90 ml) tomato juice
- 1/2 oz (15 ml) fresh lemon juice
- 1/2 oz (15 ml) Worcestershire sauce
- 2-3 dashes hot sauce (such as Tabasco)
- Pinch of salt and pepper
- Celery salt (for rimming, optional)
- Garnishes: Celery stalk, lemon wedge, olives, pickles, cooked shrimp, or any other preferred toppings
- Ice cubes

Instructions:

1. If desired, rim a highball glass with celery salt. To do this, rub a lemon wedge around the rim of the glass, then dip the rim into a shallow dish of celery salt.
2. Fill the glass with ice cubes.
3. Pour the vodka, tomato juice, fresh lemon juice, Worcestershire sauce, hot sauce, salt, and pepper into the glass.
4. Stir well to mix all the ingredients.
5. Garnish your Bloody Mary with a celery stalk and any other preferred toppings such as lemon wedge, olives, pickles, or cooked shrimp.
6. Serve and enjoy your classic Bloody Mary!

The Bloody Mary is a customizable cocktail, so feel free to adjust the ingredients to suit your taste preferences. You can also add more or less hot sauce for extra spice. Cheers!

Espresso Martini

Ingredients:

- 1 1/2 oz (45 ml) vodka
- 1 oz (30 ml) coffee liqueur (such as Kahlúa)
- 1/2 oz (15 ml) simple syrup (optional, adjust to taste)
- 1 oz (30 ml) freshly brewed espresso (cooled to room temperature)
- Coffee beans, for garnish (optional)
- Ice cubes

Instructions:

1. Fill a cocktail shaker with ice cubes.
2. Pour the vodka, coffee liqueur, simple syrup (if using), and freshly brewed espresso into the shaker.
3. Shake the ingredients vigorously for about 15-20 seconds to chill the mixture and create a frothy texture.
4. Strain the mixture into a chilled martini glass.
5. Optionally, garnish your Espresso Martini with a few coffee beans.
6. Serve and enjoy your delicious Espresso Martini!

The Espresso Martini is a sophisticated cocktail with a perfect balance of bold coffee flavor and smooth sweetness from the coffee liqueur. Adjust the sweetness by adding more or less simple syrup according to your taste preferences. Cheers!

Tom Collins

Ingredients:

- 2 oz (60 ml) gin
- 1 oz (30 ml) fresh lemon juice
- 1/2 oz (15 ml) simple syrup
- Club soda
- Lemon slice, for garnish
- Maraschino cherry, for garnish (optional)
- Ice cubes

Instructions:

1. Fill a Collins glass with ice cubes.
2. Pour the gin, fresh lemon juice, and simple syrup into the glass.
3. Stir gently to mix the ingredients.
4. Top up the glass with club soda.
5. Stir again gently to combine.
6. Garnish your Tom Collins with a lemon slice and, if desired, a maraschino cherry.
7. Serve and enjoy your classic Tom Collins!

The Tom Collins is a refreshing and effervescent cocktail with a perfect balance of tartness, sweetness, and botanical flavors from the gin. Adjust the sweetness by adding more or less simple syrup according to your taste preferences. Cheers!

Gimlet

Ingredients:

- 2 oz (60 ml) gin or vodka
- 3/4 oz (22 ml) fresh lime juice
- 1/2 oz (15 ml) simple syrup
- Lime wheel or twist, for garnish
- Ice cubes

Instructions:

1. Fill a cocktail shaker with ice cubes.
2. Pour the gin (or vodka), fresh lime juice, and simple syrup into the shaker.
3. Shake the ingredients vigorously for about 15-20 seconds to chill the mixture.
4. Strain the mixture into a chilled martini glass or a rocks glass filled with ice cubes.
5. Garnish your Gimlet with a lime wheel or twist.
6. Serve and enjoy your classic Gimlet!

The Gimlet is a simple and refreshing cocktail with a perfect balance of tartness from the lime juice and sweetness from the simple syrup, all complemented by the botanical flavors of the gin or vodka. Adjust the sweetness by adding more or less simple syrup according to your taste preferences. Cheers!

Dark 'n' Stormy

Ingredients:

- 2 oz (60 ml) dark rum
- 3-4 oz (90-120 ml) ginger beer
- 1/2 oz (15 ml) fresh lime juice
- Lime wedge, for garnish
- Ice cubes

Instructions:

1. Fill a highball glass with ice cubes.
2. Pour the dark rum over the ice.
3. Squeeze the lime juice into the glass.
4. Top up the glass with ginger beer.
5. Stir gently to combine.
6. Garnish your Dark 'n' Stormy with a lime wedge.
7. Serve and enjoy your classic Dark 'n' Stormy!

The Dark 'n' Stormy is a simple yet delicious cocktail with the spicy kick of ginger beer complementing the rich flavors of dark rum. Adjust the sweetness and tartness by adding more or less lime juice according to your taste preferences. Cheers!

Aperol Spritz

Ingredients:

- 2 oz (60 ml) Aperol
- 3 oz (90 ml) Prosecco (or any dry sparkling wine)
- Splash of soda water
- Orange slice, for garnish
- Ice cubes

Instructions:

1. Fill a wine glass or a large balloon glass with ice cubes.
2. Pour the Aperol over the ice.
3. Add the Prosecco (or sparkling wine) to the glass.
4. Give it a gentle stir to mix the Aperol and Prosecco together.
5. Top up the glass with a splash of soda water.
6. Garnish your Aperol Spritz with an orange slice.
7. Serve and enjoy your classic Aperol Spritz!

The Aperol Spritz is a refreshing and vibrant cocktail, perfect for summer sipping. Adjust the sweetness and effervescence by adding more or less soda water according to your taste preferences. Cheers!

Sidecar

Ingredients:

- 2 oz (60 ml) cognac or brandy
- 1 oz (30 ml) triple sec (such as Cointreau)
- 3/4 oz (22 ml) fresh lemon juice
- Sugar (for rimming, optional)
- Lemon twist, for garnish
- Ice cubes

Instructions:

1. If desired, rim a chilled coupe glass with sugar. To do this, moisten the rim of the glass with a lemon wedge, then dip it into a shallow dish of sugar to coat the rim.
2. Fill a cocktail shaker with ice cubes.
3. Pour the cognac (or brandy), triple sec, and fresh lemon juice into the shaker.
4. Shake the ingredients vigorously for about 15-20 seconds to chill the mixture.
5. Strain the mixture into the prepared coupe glass.
6. Garnish your Sidecar with a lemon twist.
7. Serve and enjoy your classic Sidecar!

The Sidecar is a sophisticated and timeless cocktail with a perfect balance of sweet, tart, and boozy flavors. Adjust the sweetness by adding more or less triple sec according to your taste preferences. Cheers!

White Russian

Ingredients:

- 2 oz (60 ml) vodka
- 1 oz (30 ml) coffee liqueur (such as Kahlúa)
- 1 oz (30 ml) heavy cream or milk
- Ice cubes

Instructions:

1. Fill an old-fashioned glass with ice cubes.
2. Pour the vodka and coffee liqueur over the ice.
3. Stir gently to combine.
4. Slowly pour the heavy cream or milk over the back of a spoon so that it floats on top of the mixture.
5. Give it a gentle stir to incorporate the cream into the drink.
6. Serve and enjoy your classic White Russian!

The White Russian is a creamy and indulgent cocktail with the rich flavors of vodka and coffee liqueur. Adjust the creaminess by adding more or less heavy cream or milk according to your taste preferences. Cheers!

Caipirinha

Ingredients:

- 2 oz (60 ml) cachaça (Brazilian rum)
- 1/2 lime, cut into wedges
- 2 teaspoons (8 g) granulated sugar (adjust to taste)
- Ice cubes

Instructions:

1. Place the lime wedges and granulated sugar into a rocks glass.
2. Muddle the lime and sugar together to release the lime juice and dissolve the sugar.
3. Fill the glass with ice cubes.
4. Pour the cachaça over the ice.
5. Stir well to combine and chill the drink.
6. Optionally, give the mixture a brief shake or stir.
7. Serve and enjoy your classic Caipirinha!

The Caipirinha is a refreshing and vibrant cocktail with the bright flavors of lime and the unique character of cachaça. Adjust the sweetness by adding more or less sugar according to your taste preferences. Cheers!

Mojito

Ingredients:

- 2 oz (60 ml) white rum
- 1/2 lime, cut into wedges
- 2 teaspoons (8 g) granulated sugar
- 6-8 fresh mint leaves
- Club soda (to top up)
- Ice cubes

Instructions:

1. Place the lime wedges and granulated sugar into a sturdy glass.
2. Add the fresh mint leaves to the glass.
3. Muddle the lime, sugar, and mint together gently to release the lime juice and mint oils.
4. Fill the glass with ice cubes.
5. Pour the white rum over the ice.
6. Top up the glass with club soda.
7. Stir gently to combine.
8. Optionally, give the mixture a brief shake or stir.
9. Garnish your Mojito with a sprig of fresh mint.
10. Serve and enjoy your classic Mojito!

The Mojito is a refreshing and vibrant cocktail with the perfect balance of sweetness, tartness, and minty freshness. Adjust the sweetness by adding more or less sugar according to your taste preferences. Cheers!

Piña Colada

Ingredients:

- 2 oz (60 ml) white rum
- 3 oz (90 ml) pineapple juice
- 1 oz (30 ml) coconut cream
- Pineapple wedge and maraschino cherry, for garnish
- Ice cubes

Instructions:

1. Fill a blender with ice cubes.
2. Pour the white rum, pineapple juice, and coconut cream into the blender.
3. Blend the ingredients until smooth and creamy.
4. If needed, adjust the consistency by adding more ice for a thicker texture or more pineapple juice for a thinner texture.
5. Pour the mixture into a chilled glass.
6. Garnish your Piña Colada with a pineapple wedge and maraschino cherry.
7. Serve and enjoy your classic Piña Colada!

The Piña Colada is a tropical and indulgent cocktail with the perfect blend of pineapple and coconut flavors. Adjust the sweetness by adding more or less coconut cream according to your taste preferences. Cheers!

Irish Coffee

Ingredients:

- 1 1/2 oz (45 ml) Irish whiskey
- 1 cup (240 ml) hot brewed coffee
- 2 teaspoons (8 g) brown sugar
- Heavy cream, lightly whipped
- Ground nutmeg or cocoa powder, for garnish (optional)

Instructions:

1. Preheat a heat-resistant glass or mug by filling it with hot water, then discarding the water.
2. Pour the Irish whiskey into the warmed glass.
3. Add the brown sugar to the glass.
4. Pour the hot brewed coffee over the whiskey and sugar, and stir until the sugar is dissolved.
5. Gently float a layer of lightly whipped heavy cream on top of the coffee by pouring it over the back of a spoon.
6. Optionally, garnish your Irish Coffee with a sprinkle of ground nutmeg or cocoa powder.
7. Serve and enjoy your classic Irish Coffee while hot!

The Irish Coffee is a comforting and indulgent cocktail with the warmth of whiskey and coffee, balanced by the richness of whipped cream. Adjust the sweetness by adding more or less brown sugar according to your taste preferences. Cheers!

Blue Lagoon

Ingredients:

- 1 1/2 oz (45 ml) vodka
- 1/2 oz (15 ml) blue curaçao
- 1/2 oz (15 ml) fresh lime juice
- Lemon-lime soda (such as Sprite or 7-Up)
- Lemon slice or cherry, for garnish
- Ice cubes

Instructions:

1. Fill a highball glass with ice cubes.
2. Pour the vodka and blue curaçao over the ice.
3. Squeeze the fresh lime juice into the glass.
4. Top up the glass with lemon-lime soda.
5. Stir gently to combine.
6. Optionally, garnish your Blue Lagoon with a lemon slice or cherry.
7. Serve and enjoy your refreshing Blue Lagoon cocktail!

The Blue Lagoon is a vibrant and tropical cocktail with a beautiful blue color, perfect for any occasion. Adjust the sweetness and tartness by adding more or less lime juice according to your taste preferences. Cheers!

Long Island Iced Tea

Ingredients:

- 1/2 oz (15 ml) vodka
- 1/2 oz (15 ml) white rum
- 1/2 oz (15 ml) gin
- 1/2 oz (15 ml) tequila
- 1/2 oz (15 ml) triple sec
- 1 oz (30 ml) fresh lemon juice
- 1/2 oz (15 ml) simple syrup
- Cola (to top up)
- Lemon wedge, for garnish
- Ice cubes

Instructions:

1. Fill a cocktail shaker with ice cubes.
2. Pour the vodka, white rum, gin, tequila, triple sec, fresh lemon juice, and simple syrup into the shaker.
3. Shake the ingredients vigorously for about 15-20 seconds to chill the mixture.
4. Fill a highball glass with ice cubes.
5. Strain the mixture into the glass over the ice.
6. Top up the glass with cola.
7. Stir gently to combine.
8. Garnish your Long Island Iced Tea with a lemon wedge.
9. Serve and enjoy your classic Long Island Iced Tea!

The Long Island Iced Tea is a potent and refreshing cocktail with a perfect balance of spirits and citrus flavors, topped up with cola for a hint of sweetness and effervescence. Adjust the sweetness by adding more or less simple syrup according to your taste preferences. Cheers!

Tequila Sunrise

Ingredients:

- 2 oz (60 ml) tequila
- 4 oz (120 ml) orange juice
- 1/2 oz (15 ml) grenadine syrup
- Orange slice and maraschino cherry, for garnish
- Ice cubes

Instructions:

1. Fill a highball glass with ice cubes.
2. Pour the tequila and orange juice into the glass.
3. Stir gently to combine.
4. Slowly pour the grenadine syrup into the glass over the back of a spoon. This will create a gradient effect, with the grenadine sinking to the bottom.
5. Garnish your Tequila Sunrise with an orange slice and maraschino cherry.
6. Serve and enjoy your vibrant Tequila Sunrise!

The Tequila Sunrise is a visually stunning cocktail with layers of colors resembling a sunrise, perfect for brunch or any occasion. Adjust the sweetness by adding more or less grenadine syrup according to your taste preferences. Cheers!

Sex on the Beach

Ingredients:

- 1 1/2 oz (45 ml) vodka
- 1/2 oz (15 ml) peach schnapps
- 2 oz (60 ml) cranberry juice
- 2 oz (60 ml) orange juice
- Orange slice and maraschino cherry, for garnish
- Ice cubes

Instructions:

1. Fill a highball glass with ice cubes.
2. Pour the vodka and peach schnapps into the glass.
3. Add the cranberry juice and orange juice.
4. Stir gently to combine.
5. Optionally, give the mixture a brief shake or stir.
6. Garnish your Sex on the Beach with an orange slice and maraschino cherry.
7. Serve and enjoy your fruity Sex on the Beach cocktail!

The Sex on the Beach is a colorful and fruity cocktail with a perfect blend of vodka, peach schnapps, and fruit juices, reminiscent of a tropical paradise. Adjust the sweetness by adding more or less peach schnapps according to your taste preferences. Cheers!

Hurricane

Ingredients:

- 2 oz (60 ml) light rum
- 2 oz (60 ml) dark rum
- 1 oz (30 ml) passion fruit juice
- 3/4 oz (22 ml) fresh lime juice
- 1 oz (30 ml) orange juice
- 1/4 oz (7 ml) simple syrup
- 1/4 oz (7 ml) grenadine
- Orange slice and cherry, for garnish
- Ice cubes

Instructions:

1. Fill a shaker with ice cubes.
2. Pour the light rum, dark rum, passion fruit juice, lime juice, orange juice, simple syrup, and grenadine into the shaker.
3. Shake the ingredients vigorously for about 15-20 seconds to chill the mixture.
4. Fill a hurricane glass with ice cubes.
5. Strain the mixture into the glass over the ice.
6. Optionally, garnish your Hurricane cocktail with an orange slice and cherry.
7. Serve and enjoy your tropical Hurricane cocktail!

The Hurricane is a vibrant and fruity cocktail with a perfect blend of rum, fruit juices, and sweeteners, perfect for sipping on a warm day or at a beach party. Adjust the sweetness by adding more or less simple syrup according to your taste preferences. Cheers!

Singapore Sling

Ingredients:

- 1 1/2 oz (45 ml) gin
- 1/2 oz (15 ml) cherry brandy
- 1/4 oz (7 ml) Cointreau or triple sec
- 1/4 oz (7 ml) DOM Benedictine
- 2 oz (60 ml) pineapple juice
- 3/4 oz (22 ml) fresh lime juice
- 1/4 oz (7 ml) grenadine
- A dash of Angostura bitters
- Club soda (to top up)
- Pineapple slice and cherry, for garnish
- Ice cubes

Instructions:

1. Fill a shaker with ice cubes.
2. Pour the gin, cherry brandy, Cointreau, DOM Benedictine, pineapple juice, lime juice, grenadine, and Angostura bitters into the shaker.
3. Shake the ingredients vigorously for about 15-20 seconds to chill the mixture.
4. Strain the mixture into a Collins glass filled with ice cubes.
5. Top up the glass with club soda.
6. Stir gently to combine.
7. Optionally, garnish your Singapore Sling with a pineapple slice and cherry.
8. Serve and enjoy your classic Singapore Sling!

The Singapore Sling is a complex and refreshing cocktail with a delightful blend of fruity and herbal flavors, perfect for any occasion. Adjust the sweetness by adding more or less grenadine according to your taste preferences. Cheers!

Vodka Martini

Ingredients:

- 2 1/2 oz (75 ml) vodka
- 1/2 oz (15 ml) dry vermouth
- Lemon twist or olive, for garnish
- Ice cubes

Instructions:

1. Fill a mixing glass or shaker with ice cubes.
2. Pour the vodka and dry vermouth into the glass or shaker.

Stir or shake the mixture vigorously for about 15-20 seconds to chill it.

3. (Note: Stirring is traditional for a smoother texture, while shaking adds more aeration and a slightly different texture.)
4. Strain the mixture into a chilled martini glass.
5. Garnish your Vodka Martini with a lemon twist or olive.
6. Serve and enjoy your classic Vodka Martini!

The Vodka Martini is a timeless and elegant cocktail with a simple yet sophisticated flavor profile. Adjust the amount of dry vermouth to suit your taste preferences, ranging from bone dry with just a hint to slightly wet with a bit more vermouth. Cheers!

Whiskey Smash

Ingredients:

- 2 oz (60 ml) whiskey (bourbon or rye)
- 3/4 oz (22 ml) fresh lemon juice
- 3/4 oz (22 ml) simple syrup
- 6-8 fresh mint leaves
- Lemon wheel and mint sprig, for garnish
- Crushed ice

Instructions:

1. In a mixing glass or cocktail shaker, muddle the fresh mint leaves with the lemon juice and simple syrup to release the mint oils.
2. Add the whiskey to the mixing glass.
3. Fill the mixing glass with crushed ice.
4. Shake the ingredients vigorously for about 15-20 seconds to chill the mixture.
5. Strain the mixture into a rocks glass filled with crushed ice.
6. Garnish your Whiskey Smash with a lemon wheel and mint sprig.
7. Serve and enjoy your refreshing Whiskey Smash!

The Whiskey Smash is a delightful and refreshing cocktail with the perfect balance of tartness, sweetness, and herbal notes from the fresh mint. Adjust the sweetness by adding more or less simple syrup according to your taste preferences. Cheers!

Rum Punch

Ingredients:

- 2 oz (60 ml) rum (preferably light or gold)
- 1 oz (30 ml) freshly squeezed lime juice
- 1 oz (30 ml) freshly squeezed orange juice
- 2 oz (60 ml) pineapple juice
- 1/2 oz (15 ml) grenadine syrup
- Dash of Angostura bitters (optional)
- Pineapple wedge, orange slice, and maraschino cherry, for garnish
- Ice cubes

Instructions:

1. Fill a shaker with ice cubes.
2. Pour the rum, lime juice, orange juice, pineapple juice, grenadine syrup, and Angostura bitters (if using) into the shaker.
3. Shake the ingredients vigorously for about 15-20 seconds to chill the mixture.
4. Strain the mixture into a glass filled with ice cubes.
5. Garnish your Rum Punch with a pineapple wedge, orange slice, and maraschino cherry.
6. Serve and enjoy your classic Rum Punch!

The Rum Punch is a tropical and refreshing cocktail with the perfect blend of rum, citrus juices, and grenadine syrup, reminiscent of island flavors. Adjust the sweetness by adding more or less grenadine syrup according to your taste preferences. Cheers!

White Lady

Ingredients:

- 2 oz (60 ml) gin
- 1 oz (30 ml) triple sec (such as Cointreau)
- 3/4 oz (22 ml) fresh lemon juice
- 1/2 oz (15 ml) simple syrup
- Egg white (optional)
- Lemon twist, for garnish
- Ice cubes

Instructions:

1. Fill a cocktail shaker with ice cubes.
2. Pour the gin, triple sec, fresh lemon juice, and simple syrup into the shaker.
3. Optionally, add the egg white for a frothier texture.
4. Shake the ingredients vigorously for about 15-20 seconds to chill the mixture and incorporate the egg white.
5. Strain the mixture into a chilled coupe glass.
6. Garnish your White Lady with a lemon twist.
7. Serve and enjoy your classic White Lady!

The White Lady is a sophisticated and timeless cocktail with a perfect balance of gin, triple sec, and citrus flavors, enhanced by the frothy texture from the egg white. Adjust the sweetness by adding more or less simple syrup according to your taste preferences. Cheers!

Zombie

Ingredients:

- 1 1/2 oz (45 ml) dark rum
- 1 1/2 oz (45 ml) white rum
- 1 oz (30 ml) apricot brandy
- 1 oz (30 ml) lime juice
- 1 oz (30 ml) pineapple juice
- 1/2 oz (15 ml) grenadine
- 1/2 oz (15 ml) 151-proof rum (for flaming)
- Orange slice and cherry, for garnish
- Ice cubes

Instructions:

1. Fill a shaker with ice cubes.
2. Pour the dark rum, white rum, apricot brandy, lime juice, pineapple juice, and grenadine into the shaker.
3. Shake the ingredients vigorously for about 15-20 seconds to chill the mixture.
4. Strain the mixture into a Collins glass filled with ice cubes.
5. Float the 151-proof rum on top of the drink by gently pouring it over the back of a spoon.
6. Optionally, garnish your Zombie cocktail with an orange slice and cherry.
7. Serve and enjoy your potent Zombie cocktail!

The Zombie is a strong and flavorful cocktail with a complex blend of rums, fruit juices, and grenadine, perfect for any occasion. Be cautious with the 151-proof rum, especially if you're flaming it as a garnish. Adjust the sweetness by adding more or less grenadine according to your taste preferences. Cheers, but sip cautiously!

Bellini

Ingredients:

- 2 oz (60 ml) peach puree or peach nectar
- 4 oz (120 ml) chilled prosecco or sparkling wine
- Peach slice or raspberry, for garnish (optional)
- Ice cubes (optional)

Instructions:

1. Chill a champagne flute in the refrigerator for about 15 minutes prior to serving.
2. Pour the peach puree or peach nectar into the chilled flute.
3. Slowly top up the glass with chilled prosecco or sparkling wine.
4. Gently stir to combine, being careful not to lose too much of the effervescence.
5. Optionally, add ice cubes if desired.
6. Garnish your Bellini with a peach slice or raspberry, if desired.
7. Serve and enjoy your classic Bellini!

The Bellini is a delightful and refreshing cocktail with the sweet and fruity flavor of peach complemented by the effervescence of prosecco. Adjust the sweetness by using more or less peach puree according to your taste preferences. Cheers!

French Martini

Ingredients:

- 1 1/2 oz (45 ml) vodka
- 1/2 oz (15 ml) raspberry liqueur (such as Chambord)
- 1/2 oz (15 ml) pineapple juice
- Raspberry or lemon twist, for garnish
- Ice cubes

Instructions:

1. Fill a shaker with ice cubes.
2. Pour the vodka, raspberry liqueur, and pineapple juice into the shaker.
3. Shake the ingredients vigorously for about 15-20 seconds to chill the mixture.
4. Strain the mixture into a chilled martini glass.
5. Garnish your French Martini with a raspberry or lemon twist.
6. Serve and enjoy your classic French Martini!

The French Martini is a sophisticated and fruity cocktail with the perfect balance of vodka, raspberry liqueur, and pineapple juice, creating a delightful combination of flavors. Adjust the sweetness by using more or less raspberry liqueur according to your taste preferences. Cheers!

Rob Roy

Ingredients:

- 2 oz (60 ml) Scotch whisky
- 1 oz (30 ml) sweet vermouth
- Dash of Angostura bitters
- Maraschino cherry or lemon twist, for garnish
- Ice cubes

Instructions:

1. Fill a mixing glass with ice cubes.
2. Pour the Scotch whisky, sweet vermouth, and a dash of Angostura bitters into the glass.
3. Stir the ingredients gently for about 15-20 seconds to chill the mixture and combine the flavors.
4. Strain the mixture into a chilled cocktail glass or a rocks glass filled with ice cubes.
5. Garnish your Rob Roy with a maraschino cherry or a lemon twist.
6. Serve and enjoy your classic Rob Roy!

The Rob Roy is a timeless and elegant cocktail with the rich and complex flavors of Scotch whisky and sweet vermouth, enhanced by a hint of bitters. Adjust the sweetness by using more or less sweet vermouth according to your taste preferences. Cheers!

Brandy Alexander

Ingredients:

- 1 1/2 oz (45 ml) brandy
- 1 oz (30 ml) crème de cacao (white)
- 1 oz (30 ml) cream
- Nutmeg, for garnish
- Ice cubes

Instructions:

1. Fill a shaker with ice cubes.
2. Pour the brandy, crème de cacao, and cream into the shaker.
3. Shake well until chilled.
4. Strain the mixture into a chilled cocktail glass.
5. Garnish with a sprinkle of nutmeg on top.
6. Serve and enjoy your classic Brandy Alexander!

The Brandy Alexander is a rich and creamy cocktail with a delightful blend of brandy and chocolate flavors, perfect for sipping on cozy evenings or as a dessert drink. Adjust the sweetness and creaminess by adding more or less cream according to your taste preferences. Cheers!

Black Russian

Ingredients:

- 2 oz (60 ml) vodka
- 1 oz (30 ml) coffee liqueur (such as Kahlúa)
- Ice cubes

Instructions:

1. Fill an old-fashioned glass with ice cubes.
2. Pour the vodka over the ice.
3. Add the coffee liqueur to the glass.
4. Stir gently to combine.
5. Serve and enjoy your classic Black Russian!

The Black Russian is a simple yet sophisticated cocktail with the perfect balance of vodka and coffee liqueur, creating a smooth and rich flavor profile. It's perfect for sipping as an after-dinner drink or at any social occasion. Cheers!

Irish Mule

Ingredients:

- 2 oz (60 ml) Irish whiskey
- 4 oz (120 ml) ginger beer
- 1/2 oz (15 ml) lime juice
- Lime wedge, for garnish
- Ice cubes

Instructions:

1. Fill a copper mug or highball glass with ice cubes.
2. Pour the Irish whiskey and lime juice over the ice.
3. Top up the glass with ginger beer.
4. Stir gently to combine.
5. Garnish your Irish Mule with a lime wedge.
6. Serve and enjoy your refreshing Irish Mule!

The Irish Mule is a variation of the classic Moscow Mule, substituting vodka with Irish whiskey, which adds a rich and complex flavor to the cocktail. It's a delightful and refreshing drink, perfect for any occasion. Cheers!

Aviation

Ingredients:

- 2 oz (60 ml) gin
- 1/2 oz (15 ml) maraschino liqueur
- 1/4 oz (7 ml) crème de violette
- 3/4 oz (22 ml) fresh lemon juice
- Maraschino cherry, for garnish
- Ice cubes

Instructions:

1. Fill a shaker with ice cubes.
2. Pour the gin, maraschino liqueur, crème de violette, and fresh lemon juice into the shaker.
3. Shake the ingredients vigorously for about 15-20 seconds to chill the mixture.
4. Strain the mixture into a chilled coupe glass.
5. Garnish your Aviation with a maraschino cherry.
6. Serve and enjoy your classic Aviation cocktail!

The Aviation is a classic cocktail with a delicate balance of floral, citrus, and herbal flavors, perfect for gin enthusiasts or anyone looking to try something unique and sophisticated. Adjust the sweetness by adding more or less maraschino liqueur according to your taste preferences. Cheers!

Godfather

Ingredients:

- 1 1/2 oz (45 ml) Scotch whisky
- 3/4 oz (22 ml) amaretto liqueur
- Ice cubes

Instructions:

1. Fill a mixing glass or a rocks glass with ice cubes.
2. Pour the Scotch whisky and amaretto liqueur over the ice.
3. Stir gently to combine and chill the mixture.
4. Optionally, strain the mixture into a new glass filled with fresh ice.
5. Serve and enjoy your classic Godfather cocktail!

The Godfather is a smooth and slightly sweet cocktail with the rich flavors of Scotch whisky complemented by the nutty sweetness of amaretto liqueur. It's a perfect drink for those who enjoy a balance between boldness and sweetness. Cheers!

Boulevardier

Ingredients:

- 1 1/2 oz (45 ml) bourbon or rye whiskey
- 3/4 oz (22 ml) sweet vermouth
- 3/4 oz (22 ml) Campari
- Orange twist or cherry, for garnish
- Ice cubes

Instructions:

1. Fill a mixing glass with ice cubes.
2. Pour the bourbon or rye whiskey, sweet vermouth, and Campari into the mixing glass.
3. Stir the ingredients well for about 15-20 seconds to chill and dilute the mixture.
4. Strain the mixture into a chilled cocktail glass or rocks glass filled with ice.
5. Garnish your Boulevardier with an orange twist or a cherry.
6. Serve and enjoy your classic Boulevardier cocktail!

The Boulevardier is a sophisticated and complex cocktail with a perfect balance of sweetness, bitterness, and depth of flavor. It's a great choice for whiskey lovers looking to explore new and exciting cocktails. Cheers!

Grasshopper

Ingredients:

- 3/4 oz (22 ml) green crème de menthe
- 3/4 oz (22 ml) white crème de cacao
- 3/4 oz (22 ml) heavy cream
- Mint leaf or chocolate shavings, for garnish
- Ice cubes

Instructions:

1. Fill a shaker with ice cubes.
2. Pour the green crème de menthe, white crème de cacao, and heavy cream into the shaker.
3. Shake the ingredients vigorously for about 15-20 seconds to chill the mixture.
4. Strain the mixture into a chilled cocktail glass.
5. Optionally, garnish your Grasshopper with a mint leaf or chocolate shavings.
6. Serve and enjoy your classic Grasshopper cocktail!

The Grasshopper is a delightful and indulgent cocktail with a smooth and creamy texture and a refreshing minty flavor. It's perfect for sipping as a dessert drink or on special occasions. Cheers!

Dark and Stormy

Ingredients:

- 2 oz (60 ml) dark rum
- 3 oz (90 ml) ginger beer
- 1/2 oz (15 ml) fresh lime juice
- Lime wedge, for garnish
- Ice cubes

Instructions:

1. Fill a highball glass with ice cubes.
2. Pour the dark rum over the ice.
3. Squeeze the fresh lime juice into the glass.
4. Top up the glass with ginger beer.
5. Stir gently to combine.
6. Garnish your Dark 'n' Stormy with a lime wedge.
7. Serve and enjoy your classic Dark 'n' Stormy cocktail!

The Dark 'n' Stormy is a refreshing and flavorful cocktail with the rich and spicy notes of dark rum paired with the crisp and zesty flavors of ginger beer and lime. It's perfect for sipping on a warm day or as a relaxing drink after a long day. Cheers!

www.ingramcontent.com/pod-product-compliance
Lightning Source LLC
LaVergne TN
LVHW081334060526
838201LV00055B/2644